Sorry I Pooped in Your Shoe

Sorry I Pooped in Your Shoe

(and Other Heartwarming Letters from Doggie)

Jeremy Greenberg

Andrews McMeel Publishing, LLC

Kansas City • Sydney • London

Andrews McMeel Publishing, LLC
an Andrews McMeel Universal company
1130 Walnut Street, Kansas City, Missouri 64106
www.andrewsmcmeel.com

13 14 15 SDB 10 9 8 7 6 5

ISBN: 978-1-4494-0789-6
Library of Congress Control Number: 2011926184

www.jeremygreenberg.com

ATTENTION: SCHOOLS AND BUSINESSES
Andrews McMeel books are available at quantity discounts with bulk purchase for educational, business, or sales promotional use. For information, please e-mail the Andrews McMeel Publishing Special Sales Department:
specialsales@amuniversal.com

HUGE THANKS to the extremely talented photographers who blessed this book with their work:

Valerie Abbott, Marley, page 18; Amy Burgess, Dodger, page 49; Alana Carlin, Jasper, page 29; Ruth Cassidy, Doesn't Like Dress-up, page 41; Robert Counselman, Max, page 54; Michael Culver, T-Bone, page 42; Elaine Dudzinski, Ozzy, page 33; Cindy Fike, Kellan, page 27; Peta Flemming, Samson, page 9; Jennifer Heffner, Samuel, page 45; Carolyn Abell Hodges, Macy, page 26; Davee Hughes, Frogdog, page 25; Peggy Hughes, Mario, page 34; Lin Jia, Gandalf, page 10; Erin Leonard, Raisin, page 62; Caroline Li, Mousse, page 50; Matt Mallett, Bernie, page 37; Sarah Novak, Jane, page 30; Jodi Payne, Sammy, page 38; Ellen Pierce, Doll, page 58; Rebecca Pizzo Photography, Mr. P Nut, page 14; Paula Rivas, Biting the Colors, page 21; Kathleen Slovachek, Dante, page 6; Marshall Stokes, Stella, page 53; Renee Tellez, Mel, page 22; Reggie Thibodeau, Jewel, page 13; Valerie Trinidad, Babe, page 57; Bernadette Walsh, Spike, page 46; Marit Welker, Sukie, page 6.

From: Sukie
Age: 5 Years
Re: I heard there was a reward for a lost shoe

Dear Pack Leader,

I couldn't help but notice you running around the house frantically looking for one of your $200 running shoes. Perhaps I can be of assistance. I smelled, er, uh, saw the shoe buried under my dog toys. In situations like these, it's best not to ask questions and just be thankful to have the shoe back. Unfortunately, I can't guarantee its condition. When shoes that smell so scrumptiously like Pack Leader's feet are abducted, they often have some bite or chew marks. If you find that the shoe is damaged beyond use, I will graciously accept it as my reward for returning it to you.

Love,
Sukie

Dear Pack Leader,

Thank you for throwing this ball into the lake! I love retrieving it almost as much as I love shaking frigid lake water all over you afterward. And even though it's not a duck, I will still enjoy sneaking it into the house later to rip off its fuzz.

Some doggies have to learn to swim, but I was bred to retrieve. So if you ever get bored, just know that in addition to fetching a tennis ball from a lake, I will gladly dive for rubber rings in a swimming pool, fetch stones out of the ocean, snatch the baby's bath toys from the tub, and even remove those big, funny goldfish from the neighbor's little pond.

Love,
Samson

From: Samson
Age: 4 Years
Re: Honestly, I was gonna jump in whether you threw the ball or not

From: Gandalf
Age: 2 Years
Re: Maybe I have one in my purse

Dear Pack Leader,

What is that thing with four legs that just walked by us on the ground? It smelled like another doggie, but that can't be—it wasn't being carried around in a leather purse. Is it true that some doggies aren't allowed to go on airplanes? What about the rumor that not all doggies eat standing on a dining room table? That sounds too impossible to be true. And please tell me those stories about doggies who pull people through the snow are just tales told to puppies at night before they go to sleep on their pillow-top mattress doggie beds. I mean, humans pulling doggies makes sense. You carry me everywhere. But a doggie hauling around humans? Do you know how big of a purse you'd need?

Love,
Gandalf

Dear Sprinkler Head,

First of all, I respect you as I respect all great adversaries. Sprinkler Head is second only to Vacuum Cleaner in terms of ferocity. No matter how hard Jewel bites Sprinkler Head's stream of water, Sprinkler Head keeps turning and sprinkling. My pack leader says I'm a dumb doggie, that Jewel can never figure out Sprinkler Head's tactics. But she underestimates Sprinkler Head. I'm always surprised when Sprinkler Head pops out of the ground. Sprinkler Head waits till I'm stuck in crouching potty position, knows I'm vulnerable for attack, then pops out of the ground and Sprinkler Head does business on Jewel while Jewel does business on lawn.

But we're not finished, Sprinkler Head. One day I will bite your stream of water just right and you will shut off and retreat, knowing that Jewel has victoriously defended herself against an irrigation system.

Your worthy opponent,
Jewel

From: Mr. P Nut
Age: 12 Years
Re: That's Mr. P Nut to you

Dear Beloved Pack Leader,

Why am I so grumpy? Because despite my name clearly being Mr. P Nut, just as it says on my tag, you and the rest of the pack repeatedly laugh as you call me Mr. P-Diddy Dingleberry, Nutsy-P Nutter, Mr. Pee-pee Nut, The Vet Cut Off His P Nuts, Mr. P Nuts and Popcorn, Mr. P Has Gone Nuts, and perhaps the worst of all, Mr. Allergic to P Nuts. You know I love you, Pack Leader, but think about how you'd feel if instead of calling you Marsha I called you Swamp Marsha, Drain the Marsha, or Damp Marsha? You'd be sitting on the grass making an adorably grumpy face as well.

My great granpaw, the original Mr. P Nut (who spelled it Peaznutten until he went through Ellis Island) came to this country in search of a better dog park. And I am proud to have the Mr. P Nut name.

I understand you can't undo years of calling me names like Mr. P Nutty Nutcracker overnight. But if you ask me if I want a cookie, I think that we can start the healing process.

Love,

Mr. P Nut the Third, Esq.

Dear Pack Leader,

Even though I'm a little puppy, I know my manners. If someone's kind enough to pour you a glass of red stuff, you should drink it. Normally German shepherds aren't into red drink, but I know humans have it all the time, so it would be rude of me not to at least taste it. So far I've tasted down to the length of my tongue. I left the rest for you, because I know it's nice to share.

If you want to go back in the kitchen and get me a, how do you say, *sandwich*, I will politely sample that as well.

Love,
Kellan

From: Kellan
Age: 3 Months
Re: Well, if you insist

From: Marley
Age: 2 Years
Re: Piggy told me what you said about me

Dear Pack Leader,

Just because I'm happy-go-lucky by nature doesn't mean I don't have feelings. Piggy told me that you said you thought I was cuter as a puppy. Well, I'm sure there are people who thought you were cuter when you were younger. But if I was your puppy back then, I wouldn't say mean things about you if you suddenly grew a fatty tumor on your hind leg, or only had eyebrows over one eyeball. I could look past your mangy appearance and see your inner beauty.

This has made me so sad that Piggy and I are refusing to get out of bed this morning. I know you have to go to work, but you really hurt my feelings. It's not like you're a spring chicken (or I'd eat you—spring chicken is Marley's favorite flavor of dog food).

Piggy says you owe me an apology. And please apologize soon. I really have to pee.

Love,
Marley

Dear Beloved Beta,

Okay, I'll go over the rules one more time: First I bring you the ball, then you say, "Out!" which I think means "tug." You try to remove the ball from my mouth while I clench down. Then you repeat, "Out, Lua" while I completely fail to understand you, and maybe also let out a few playful growls. Then you say, "Lua, let go" while I wag my tail because I heard my name. Finally, after you give up and let go, I make sure the ball is drenched in slobber and then drop it in your lap, just to grab it away again when you reach for it.

Please try to keep up! This is an important game that helps us establish pack order, and I can't continue to outrank you if you won't play.

Love,
Lua

From: Lua
Age: 4 Years
Re: You can take the ball, but I want you to earn it

From: Mel
Age: 6 Years
Re: Don't clean the house—I just stank it up!

Dear Pack Leader,

I don't spend all day putting my adorable Mel stink all over the carpet so you can run in here with your loud windbag friend and remove it. Don't you want people to know that you have a dog the moment they walk in the door? I work very hard to make sure that everything you own smells like Mel. As your doggie, it's my job to provide an environment that profoundly stinks like an old mutt who hasn't had a bath in six months. I would appreciate a bit of consideration for the work I do.

Oh, and make sure you leave your shoes on when you come in this house, so I know where you've been!

Love,
Smelly Mel

Dear Pack Leader,

Look, we all have days when things don't go smoothly. I know that you're embarrassed. I can see you turning away and trying to pretend I'm someone else's doggie. But this is no different than when you're in the bathroom and have to yell out for someone to bring you more toilet paper. I don't pretend to not know you when that happens. In fact, I try to get into the bathroom when the door opens just to hang out with you in your time of need.

And this doesn't mean we have to go to the vet. I don't have impacted anal glands, and I don't have worms. I don't have an allergy, and I don't have a tick.

I just have poor timing.

Why don't you stop hiding your face, grab some leaves, and give me a hand.

Love,
Your Frogdog

From: Frogdog
Age: 6 Years
Re: A clean break with the past

From: Macy

Age: 7 Months

Re: We never go out anymore (and I'm sorry I pooped in your shoe)

Dear Pack Leader,

I'll never forget the day you adopted me. You looked at me and said, "Yes. This one will work." And it was wonderful. We used to go out all the time. You'd come home from work and look me in the eyes and say, "Okay, Macy. Do your magic." And we'd walk by all the cute girls at the coffee shops and the yogurt shops. And then one day a woman bent down to scratch my cute head and said, "Hi. I'm Penny." Ever since, you and Penny have been like kibbles and bits. But I barely get a ball thrown at me and am no longer allowed on your bed. I am beginning to feel like you used me just to get a girlfriend! You probably even named me Macy just because women like that department store.

I'm not asking you to leave Penny in the car on a hot day. But since we never go out anymore, I didn't think you'd mind if I pooped in your shoe.

Love,
Macy

Dear Pack Leader,

Did you hear that? There's a ghost in the closet! I know you said, "Jasper, relax. It's just something that fell." But why would something just fall? After I'm done being surprised, I will bark and growl at it again. I know you said, "Jasper, it's just a jacket sliding off the hanger. Stop barking and chew on your bone." But who can chew at a time like this? I wonder if it's the same ghost who you're convinced is just the ice maker. It would make sense—it's got to get cold making all that ice, so the ghost probably needs a jacket.

Love,
Jasper

From: Jasper
Age: 6 Months
Red: This house is haunted!

From: Jane
Age: 11 Years
Re: I love the smell of summer and a decomposing squirrel

Dear Pack Leader,

Here's a bit of advice: If you want people to like you, then you have to routinely rub your body on decaying animals. For example, if you have a hot date, nothing beats a good roll in the festering remains of a squirrel. It's an immediate attention getter! For family functions, I recommend mashing your fur into the putrid carcass of a dead bird. Its delicate aroma will not be immediately noticeable when you trot into the room, but you'll soon leave everyone breathless! A good workplace stench shouldn't be too strong, so go with a bit of dead mouse. It will provide just a hint of gag-inducing funk, yet still leave everyone asking, "What did you roll in?"

And please don't feel self-conscious if you don't stink like a festering rodent. I still love you.

Love,
Jane

Dear Pack Leader,

Why do I look so adorably sad? Because I clearly heard you tell one of the younger pack members to *park* it! Then you told an older pack member that you were going to teach him how to parallel *park*, after you finished watching your favorite movie, *Gosford Park*. Every doggie knows what the word *park* means. Yet, you don't seem to be putting your shoes on. I even did my flailing French bulldog sprint to the door, complete with a near hyperventilating pant. But you just looked at me and asked, "What is it, Ozzy? Chill out."

Sure, Ozzy will chill. It's okay. And the next time you say, "Ozzy, come," I'll ignore you because I'm sure you just meant "I'd like some gum."

Love,
Ozzy

From: Ozzy
Age: 1 Year
Re: Yes, I would love to go to the *parallel park*!

From: Mario
Age: 4 Years
Re: My pack leader kindly requests that you get off her ass

Dear Other Pack Leader,

I'm introducing myself because, according to my pack leader, you are riding our asses so closely that you must want to get to know us. Well, I want to get to know you, too! My pack leader also says we're surrounded by idiots. Nice to meet you, idiot! My name's Mario.

I love learning about other people. You must be very educated, because all of my pack keeps asking who in the hell taught you how to drive. I wish I could drive, but I'm a doggie.

This traffic jam is a lot of fun. It's like a dog park for cars. It's neat to see so many people who, according to my pack leader, drive with their heads up their asses. What a great way to get to know yourself!

Love,
Mario

Howdy, Beta Buddy,

Whatcha doin'? Me, I'm in the backyard. Alpha sent me out here because she said she was trying to clean. So, then I stuck my nose through the knot in the piece of fence and chatted with the neighbor's dog for a while. But then someone yelled, "Shut up, Bernie!" and the other dog went inside its house. Then I climbed onto the sun chair and napped for a bit, until I heard the door open, and I figured Alpha must've thrown you out, too. So I was thinking that we should totally hang. If you're going to wash your car, I am more than happy to attack the hose. If you want to cut the grass, I can walk behind you and bark at the mower. Are you going to put up Christmas lights? I can make you nervous by running back and forth under the ladder. Come on, Beta. I wanna do something! I'm bored, man! I even offered Alpha to help clean the house, but apparently licking the metal banister had already been done.

Love,
Bernie

From: Bernie
Age: 8 Years
Re: Howdy, Beta Buddy

From: Sammy
Age: 2 Years
Re: Always leave 'em smiling

Dear Pack Leader,

I just want to take a moment and let you know how lucky I am to have such a thoughtful companion. Most doggies have to hunt leaves one by one. But you conveniently rake them into little hills all around the yard. You even yell, "Sammy, I just raked those!" to let me know that they're ready for me to jump into and rescatter all over the yard. And you further cheer me on by yelling, "Sammy, come on!"

You know, I used to get a bit jealous when you'd set out warm, clean clothes fresh from the dryer for the cat to sit on. But that's just one pile of clothes. You must've made like four or five piles of leaves for me! I will show my gratitude later by barking at the doorbell while the kids are napping. In the meantime, I'll go in the house while you re-rake the leaves.

Love,
Sammy

Dear Pack Leader Dearest,

I'm sorry I didn't make Prima Doggie Ballerina, Mama. I'll try harder, I promise. I know that you had a bright future as a dancer until you decided to settle down and adopt puppies. You gave it all up for me, and one day I'll get that lead in the *Pupcracker* and make you so proud. I don't wanna go to the park like the other puppies my age. I have an opportunity to be something, just like you used to. I'll work extra hard to balance on my hind legs when you hold a piece of hot dog above my nose. It's the least I can do for your getting me this beautiful tutu.

Love,
Camilla

From: Camilla
Age: 8 Months
Re: Purina Ballerina

Dear Pack Leader,

Quick question: When you were growing up did your mommy make you eat on a welcome mat by yourself in a corner of the house? Bet not. She probably set your bowl on the table next to the other pack members. So why do you make me eat alone on the floor like I'm some kind of dog?

I love you, and I'm a pack animal. I'm not some antisocial cat or serial killer. I would very much appreciate it if you placed my bowl next to yours. It's important to my self-esteem. Plus, doggies who don't get to eat with humans are at greater risk of becoming Alpoholics. So please let me sit with you during dinner, or I'll spend the rest of my life thinking that I'm just some pet.

Love,
T-Bone

Dear Pack Leader,

For a limited time only, I will be giving out free dog kisses. This is a special promotion, so don't wait. The details are as follows: Anyone who is part of my pack who happens to walk too closely to me will be given one free, remarkably sloppy dog kiss on her leg. Any baby crawling by me on the ground will be given a slobbery kiss across his face, as well as near the mouth—just in case there are any spare food crumbs. Pack members who fall asleep with their feet sticking out of a blanket will receive free, ticklishly-yucky toe kisses. And anyone who lets me sit on her lap will be given a big, wet, spittle-filled smooch.

Remember to act now! This special only lasts until you say, "Samuel, that is sooooo disgusting. Knock it off!"

Love,
Samuel

From: Samuel
Age: 7 Years
Re: Free dog kisses for a limited time only

From: Spike
Age: 6 Years
Re: Help me help you

Dear Pack Leader,

You look tired! You know what helps my tail wag after a long day of not being near you? Repeatedly dropping Squeak Doggie-Dog in your lap until you look at me and yell, "How many times do I have to throw this nasty thing?!" Every day you leave for what in dog years feels like a week. I get to stay home and gnaw on Squeakeezy. But you have to be away at someplace that makes your shoes smell like cheap carpet. I bet you dream about throwing this toy for me all day long. Well, I am not the kind of doggie who will just walk away after having my Squeak Doggie-Dog thrown once! I love you! And I won't stop bringing you the Squeak-O Double D until you scream, "Enough, Spike!" and throw it in a drawer.

Then I'll just stare at you.

Love,
Spike

Dear Pack Leader,

Since I'm your "Am I ready to have a baby?" tester puppy, I thought you'd appreciate a brief progress report:

You call me "Dodger Wodger" about 7.5 times per day—an excellent level of cutesy baby talk! I can really see you doing that to a human baby and it actually caring, even if you didn't have a cookie in your hand. And you've already set up playdates with the next-door neighbor's puppy. That is thoughtful but not necessary. Since that doggie and I are neighbors, I can assure you that unless you reinforce every piece of the shared fence, that puppy and I will have many playdates without your having to arrange them.

Obviously you're doing an amazing job with toys and blankets. This fuzzy banana thing is at exactly my sleep number. And while this stuffed-crab toy's a bit weird, I'm guessing it was a gift from a well-meaning uncle who works at the seafood counter of a grocery store, so I'm willing to let it go.

So keep up the great work! I'd say right now the only difference between me and a human baby is my ability to tap a paw on the back door when I need to go potty.

Love,
Baby Dodger

From: Dodger
Age: 12 Weeks
Re: Human baby simulation almost complete

From: Mousse
Age: 3 Years
Re: It doesn't have to be like this; you're making a mistake

Dear Wannabe Groomer Pack Leader,

Can we talk about this? I'm not that dirty, I promise! I know some doggies love baths. But some doggies also eat their own poop. If I'd known this was why you called me, I would've gone limp and forced you to drag me into the tub. I can't believe I didn't see this coming. I guess your starting to brush me should've been my first clue. When I saw the towels, I thought that maybe you were taking a bath. That's fine. I'll wait outside the tub and lick the water off of your legs when you get out. But then you pulled out the giant orange bottle of doggie soap, with that dumb smiling bulldog.

That bulldog on the cover of the shampoo bottle seems happy to be bathed because she doesn't have a naturally shiny, beautiful coat. Most bulldogs aren't into appearance. But Mousse is a pretty doggie! Please don't give me a bath. My fur will get so dry and frizzy that you'll think I'm a Lakeland terrier.

Love,
Mousse

Dear Pack Leader,

Why are you constantly yelling, "Stella! Stella! Stop barking!"?
I bark way less than the rest of the pack. Other pack members are
always barking about how their day in school was, or for me to
stop drinking from the toilet. But I bark only when I absolutely have
to: like when I have to use the potty, when I want my breakfast,
or when the doorbell rings, or another dog walks by the house,
or the cat gives me a dirty look from atop the staircase, or I see
my reflection in a mirror, or Timmy falls down a well, or if I need to
practice my singing for the next full moon.

I'm practically giving you the silent treatment.

Love,
Stella

From: Stella
Age: 6 Years
Re: I think the mail's here!

From: Max
Age: 18 Months
Re: You said, "Not on the couch." This *isn't* the couch.

Dear Pack Leader,

I don't know why you're looking at me like that. I clearly recall you saying, "Max, get off the couch!" And that's why I'm on the recliner. I know you didn't expect me to curl up on the floor. It's covered in dog hair. Yuck! But this recliner has no hair on it, and it smells like you—my favorite smell in the whole world.

Please don't make me get down. Do you know how much work it was to get up here? I forgot this is a rocking chair, and when I jumped up the first time, it flew backward and scared the crap out of me. I had to growl at the chair for an hour before trying again. And now that I've finally settled in, I really do not want to get down—unless I can have a spot on the couch.

Love,
Max

Dear Pack Leader,

Seriously, I totally thought this was one of my Beggin' Strips. Whoops! Honest mistake. I know that I am only allowed to eat from your plate when you're in the other room. But here you are, right in front of me, and boy do I almost have egg on my face.

This is really just a big misunderstanding. I would never take something that I thought was yours if I thought you'd catch me. In the future, I will try to do a better job listening for the difference between the sound your shoes make on the kitchen linoleum and on the family room's hardwood. I apologize for being caught stealing your bacon, and I promise not to get caught in the future.

Love,
Babe

From: Babe
Age: 2 Years
Re: Let's play "Steal the Bacon"

From: Doll
Age: 14 Years
Re: The scent of a woman

Dear Beloved Pack Leader,

I know I shouldn't be on the bed, but I just want to sleep in your wonderful scent. Not every doggie has a leader who smells of Paris Hilton brand perfume and Lady Speed Stick, and I want to enjoy it! You always make me sleep on the little bed on the floor, and I like that bed—don't get me wrong. It even has my name embroidered on it. But it smells like cedar chips. My pack leader is not a tree!

You clearly aren't aware of how delightful it is to sleep in another doggie's funk, or you'd let me on the bed with you every night. That's why I'm rubbing myself on your sheets. Now, when you go to bed tonight, all you'll be able to think about is me.

Love,
Doll

Dear Pack Leader,

I know what you're thinking, but this isn't just another one of my yearly attempts to enjoy the cheesy popcorn that Uncle Karl sends at Christmas. I actually have a surprise for you! I'm training to be a Seeing Eye dog. I know there are schools for that. But first, I thought putting this tin on my head would help me understand what it's like not to see. The fact that there were cheesy popcorns at the bottom, which I did eat, was purely a coincidence.

Now if you'd be so kind, please help me get this thing off my head, or I'll need my own guide dog to keep from banging into the couch.

Love,
Dante

From: Dante
Age: 15 Years
Re: It's not what it looks like

From: Raisin
Age: 18 Months
Re: That bag of feathers was, like, impossible to open

Dear Pack Leader,

You know, as pack leaders go, you don't get enough credit for the small things you do to make me happy. Even when you don't say, "You wanna go, Raisin?" and take me with you, you know that I'll get bored alone, so you graciously leave a homemade bag of feathers for me to play with. Thank you!

But if you don't mind a bit of constructive criticism, you really should've left one side of the bag open. I had to tear at it for like an hour to get to the feathers. Only after digging my rear claws into the couch as an anchor was I finally able sever the bag that I've watched you work on ever since Raisin was a little puppy Raisinette.

Also, for the next feather bag you make me, can you leave the feathers on the bird?

Love,
Raisin

Acknowledgments

First and foremost, allow me give the absolute highest thanks again to this book's brilliant editor, Lane Butler, for believing in my profound mission to make fun of stuff. Also, a world of thanks to my awesome agent, David Fugate, for insisting I pitch this idea. Super huge thanks to Caty Neis for graciously reading gazillions of e-mails and helping me evaluate photos; to Kathy Hilliard for her outstanding promotional work; and to everyone at Andrews McMeel who have again devoted themselves to the creation of another great book!

Very special thanks to everyone at team MSN: to the amazing Gina Cohen and her tireless efforts to build our family of readers; to Nicole Ghazal for getting it all started; and to everyone else at Lifestyle and beyond who have continued to make room for *The Family Room*.

I would further like to thank Amanda Brothers of Sidekick Dog Training, Molly Wyman, my sherpa Chris Federico, Andrew Norelli, Tommy Savitt, and all of my great friends and colleagues!

And, most important, my deepest love and thanks to my beautiful wife, Barbara; our amazing children, Ben and Seth; and my doggie and muse, Dagny.